A BOW FORGED FROM ASH

A BOW FORGED FROM ASH

MELISSA POWLESS DAY

Palimpsest Press
1171 Eastlawn Ave.
Windsor, Ontario. N8S 3J1
www.palimpsestpress.ca

Printed and bound in Canada
Cover design and book typography by Ellie Hastings
Edited by Jim Johnstone

Palimpsest Press would like to thank the Canada Council for the Arts and the Ontario Arts Council for their support of our publishing program. We also acknowledge the assistance of the Government of Ontario through the Ontario Book Publishing Tax Credit.

Canada

LIBRARY AND ARCHIVES CANADA CATALOGUING IN PUBLICATION

TITLE: A bow forged in ash / Melissa Powless Day.
NAMES: Powless Day, Melissa, author.
IDENTIFIERS: Canadiana (print) 20250245299
Canadiana (ebook) 20250247747

ISBN 9781997508038 (SOFTCOVER)
ISBN 9781997508045 (EPUB)
SUBJECTS: LCGFT: Poetry.
CLASSIFICATION: LCC PS8631.O85 B69 2025 | DDC C811/.6—DC23

To Pixie
Miigwetch for everything you taught me. Baa maa pi.

Table of Contents

Nock

Pull

Loose

NOCK

Northern Lights

Pitch black cold …
December?
Nogojiwanong.

I remember the warmth of your hand.

The warmth in our throats
A beautiful roar
of women making
thunder

We are not afraid, you told me.
This is us reclaiming.

That deep night protest –
voices, electric
buzzing,
willful.

When late hours caught up with little legs, you put me on your shoulders.

Breaching the crowd …
surfacing
bright hats and scarves, people
undulating.

Pinks, yellows, greens – dancing light meant to ward away wendigos. We were vibrations to sunder silences.

I was too young
to understand then,
        why we needed medicine
        the foreboding of the night

To me,
You conjured Wawatay and set me on its back.

That's how I knew,
You
were magic.

Moccasin Poem

bezhig.

This deer skin
become a moccasin
of deer skin, this shoe

is the colour
of earth (no,
earth is the colour
of this deer skin shoe).

The porcupine quills
are gone, the
foot is gone, the
great, round drum
is gone;

this deer skin was
shaped by the drum
of the Earth.

niizh.

This moccasin in my office

where I begin
this poem   was

hidden in an attic
found (this moccasin,
this poem).

Cut to a function,
this deer skin was
(the foot is   gone-

nswi.

Beige, rabbit-toed,
the jingle dress shoe

taken from the dancer or
a child crying   shed it in
the Sixties Scoop or
a mother   kept it in
the Voortman's cookie tin or

it is a million
songs older than
the foot that
chased deer or
danced medicine
steps (or chants) or

niinan.

This moccasin
was lost.

In the attic
my grandmother
kept
to herself

my mother
kept to herself

naanan.

It is deer skin
old as the last
Hunt, the
forbidden/the
formidable hunt,
the forbidden
drum, the
forbidden Indians

(the wiingashk shines
golden (infrequently
the bullrush the
peaches & cream corn the
wetlands reeds shine
golden along the Bkejwanong
shore (the
frybread   summer

ngodwaaswi.

This deer skin shoe
stopped a finger
long enough for one
What the

The Anishinaabe (the
Potawatomi?) not

finding the mocc
cursed.

?did she curse
?did she try to
go back
?what happened
I have to/I want
to know (not know)
?WHAT HAPPENED
?(to the other mocc)

niizhwaaswi.

The poem
is the deer skin
measured and sewn
until it is shaped
like the waawaashkeshi skin
moccasin, the shoe

nshwaaswi.

Now the attic is
mine because
I inherited it
(for a price)

from an old woman
(with a grown daughter)
who always

knew that the land
did not belong

to the white guy who
gave it to the Queen
(for a price) who
gave it to the City of London
(for a price) which
gave it to another Shaagnaash
(for a price) who
gave it to my mother
(2k under asking
Jeez I painted
all the rooms I
did all the floors) who

gave it to her daughter
(who had it taken away)

zhaangswi.

This won't
surprise you.

My grandmother
loved the moccasin.

mdaaswi.

My great grandmother (on her deathbed)
told stories.
She sung in her sleep.
She drank one glass of Ensure
each morning.
She was keen
for life.
She was keen for the
sunlight on her face, the smell
of sweetgrass, the distant
orchestra of bineshiiyag,
the memories she carried, the touch
of a black ash strip in her slim fingers.

She was keen for her many
sons and granddaughters,
for her baskets, for her own
garden and kitchen and
her own dog and cat.

She found the moccasin
on a forage in the
eastern corner of what
she knew as
the rez.

She kept it (the
moccasin) in each telling
of how she made
her black ash baskets.

mdaaswi shaa bezhig.

I keep it
on my desk
(the moccasin).

Sometimes I play with it
in the sunlight
(to kick up thoughts)

smelling a little of (sweet)
grass or maybe even of
drying baapaagimaak or of
drum beats loud
in the morning sun.

Displace

This place sits on a salmon's back
fighting currents, fish and waterfalls
run red, bloodied – the world tears at his scales,
drinks in his blood –
just to survive

This place sits between definition & opposition
scrawling infinity in an ampersand –
a gradation cut so finely it slivers us all,
so sharp
razor thin
your fingers run red each time you fall & claw to get back up again

What blood is this, you ask
and I say,
we are all caught
red-handed

This place is a colony, an island
a corner of a page torn away
a chunk of earth that strayed too far – got caught in an orbit not of its own making

Who made this place?
Just listen.

Debwewin. Debwewin. Debwewin.

This place is a broken algorithm
with no fixed point in space
a trajectory over-determined by
past lies & future truths
stories that harden our bodies against the gravity of the world

This place is the cedar in the winter and the cedar in the summer
the drumline
the honour beat
without it, there are no songs to sing

That place we are swimming to?
Debwewin. Debwewin. Debwewin.
Our truth.

Refraction

Driving down the 401
your hands on the wheel
me, anticipating

The way the sun would glint
catch the pink
the blue
the way they rose up

My glass castles

You never told me they were office buildings.

Instead, you said
"Tell me about them"

We built stories
… knights & dragons
pegasus & unicorns …
driving through
Tkaronto

Now I sit beside you
laughing

I want to remember the laughing.

The last thing we'll do
is (hold hands)
and I'll sing your favourite songs

Me, in a chair
shaking
scared

Your hands on my shoulders
Your voice, calm

the teacher
wanted me gone
the school
wanted me gone

You didn't believe their lies.

Instead, you looked them in the eye
and said
"No"

Out on the sidewalk
You swore …
(*You never swore like that before!*)
"Never let them see you angry"

"They love to see us angry"

Hunched over
aching
I stand up

You reach over the rails
and rub my back

"Are you alright"
You ask

Shouldn't I be asking you that?

Sledding
You, holding me tight
us taking flight

Stomachs in our throats
snow in the face
screaming
joy

We should have bailed.

Instead, we crashed
Your leg tangled in the chain link fence

I loosened boot laces
(Small hands, slender fingers)

I saved you that day

I'm sitting here
staring, waiting
Where are you?

I play with plastic cups
and pink hospital swabs
stacking

When they roll you in
they roll their eyes
(See?)

I made you a castle.

Instead, you laugh
"What kind of mother raised you"

Good question.

This is not a discovery

There is a gravity to you
a pit of pull
full and empty
a promise
waiting to be filled – water filling a glass

There is a gravity to us
solid ground to hold us
stand firm against the shifting sands our toes cannot grasp
Do we pull the world or does the world pull us?

The Earth spews lightning –
(giving life to electrons as they crackle across the sky)
laughs thunder, rumbles continents

We must be content
with the whisper of our voices
as it dances from our breath
disrupting airwaves, one vibration   at a time

There is a gravity in me
(a neutron star that tugs at turtles, presses cinders into birch)
beats with the steps of
a round dance

This gravity
pulls at the water in our veins
makes tides out of decision and regret
rights us when we capsize
so that we float instead

It was the gravity in them that they knew their way through the stars, you know

This gravity has caught all the memories and medicine
that fell from our hands
suspended, they rest

Waiting to be picked up again.

Blood Memory

A People, cut
bleed
– not feather and beads
or stoic glances, but –
generations

Deep arterial spray
thick with stolen babies and miseducation

When Nokomis says Nanda emkwaan
wanting sugar for her tea
those words are bandages
staving off lingual exsanguination …

My daughter (will pack the wound)
I pack the wound.
My mother (packs the wound)
Nokomis grins that knowing grin

Our pack work is a patchwork
a quilt
stitching together evidence, resistance
with thick threads of resilience
– Boozhoo and fry bread, big drum singers and Elijah Harper
– Cindy Blackstock and those Bear Clan Patrollers …

We have 30 000 years of blood in our veins, you know.

When I venture out into the cold
I wrap our quilt around my shoulders
and slip on
my mother's moccasins

To walk
as we have always done
in the footsteps of those who came before
and those who have yet to come

Bezhgoozhi

Time doesn't stop on Walpole, just flows differently. A river melting into a lake – there's more room where there's more history. Currents hot and cold, fast and slow can spread their arms and legs, can dance and mingle with the old waters, the deep waters. Time on Walpole is like blue becoming green.

August sunlight is the colour of elder bullrush, not gold but something richer amidst the upstart greens that drift with us. The brown spikes are these beings' heads and they watch us with a stalky sway. A thousand eyes called seeds packed atop a single reed. In the fall, how many secrets rest in the wishes children blow into the wind?

Do they know where the horses went?

We came here in our childhood, searching for bezhgoozhi. The nektosha of the Pottowatomi. Those wild things Shaagnaash called mustangs. All fire and prairie running free on our Walpole whirlpool island.

Do those legs know how to stop?

Fish gotta swim. A bird's gotta fly. Horses are meant to run.

We saw one once, through the grasses and cat-tailed keepers. First, shimmers of sound and motion, drumbeats against the earth. Then, a flash of copper. Reeds. She stood before us, a mare that called the wind with her hooves, and billowed along the shoreline, churning sand and water as one. Bezhgoozhi.

Now, the sand is still. Beach and waters only meet. We skim here to the shallows, wading with bullrush, trolling for glimpses we've already seen.

But when she spoke to us, she reared, and we saw how humans grew from horses, how our bodies bloomed from their strong backs, how our thighs were meant for clinging, their manes meant for grasping, two beings breathing, beating thunder into dirt.

We're almost through the shoal, Keegan breathes, nodding to the thinning crowds of brown-eyed watchers. Young and old defend the shore, warpoles for four-leggeds that ripple through the ebb and flow of rivers, lakes and two cousins' search for wild. We never told a soul about her.

What are bullrush meant for anyway? Keegan mutters. Where gritty, salty disappointment used to sit, there is, now, a bitter resignation in the gut. The way butterflies need their dust, wings cannot be touched, bezhgoozhi cannot stop, running is what keeps her alive. She will always run and we will always look, but looking doesn't mean we're meant to find.

What are bullrush meant for?

Catching things the wind no longer carries, slowing boats, hiding from cousins the reason why Grams complain of horsehair when our own manes need braiding.

Moccasin Walk

Moccasins?
Don't talk to me about moccasins

I remember
A hot afternoon
Sun searing the sidewalk
And me
Walking with my auntie
In my moccasins

I loved those moccasins
Soft deer hide
Stretched just … right
Feeling the heat of the ground under (Indian) feet
I could run like a rabbit through grass in those moccs
I was proud
  To wear them

But I grew so fast
Knobby knees
Spindly legs

My mother had to give them away
There's someone who needs these now, she said
Ok, I said
I knew
Someone else deserved a chance to
  Feel the warmth of the earth rise up through their (Indian) feet
  Run like waabooz
  Walk proud in their moccasins.

Now they sell them at Ardene
Polyester and acrylic
Faux fur fluffed around the top

Settlers ask,
Should I wear these moccasins to the pow wow?
And I answer,
Whose auntie made them for you?

Rough Cut

My grandma understood that
the path of most resistance is sometimes silent
a song at rest

Whereas inbetween
accents might become beatings
as though the clip of a tongue
is a slip of savagery—
the click of a pen
checking boxes on a clipboard
Beat the Irish. Beat the Indian.
Beat the devil out of them.

In between the breaths
heyaa heyaww
when their boots connect to the ribs
you might remember
the capacity for bombings is not possessed
by the tongue or teeth

They can kick all they want.

Smash molars out of sockets
send incisors sailing away
with fists
that taste of flesh and blood
salt and rust

but you don't need teeth to sing.

Winter Roads

We're in a boat,
my grandfather and I,
floating on the divide
that separates Stoney/Clear Lake
and I'm bawling, blubbering, sputtering –

Grandpa is laughing, fiddling with a lure – that orange lure, the one that wriggles in the sun, catching light and flesh with barbed j-hooks. My mom hooked a bass right through the eye once, and, of course, I had to take it out. The lure snagged me on the finger, tearing red against the green lake water.

My grandfather is laughing,
wearing that bright red baseball cap.
His chuckles bounce the boat, and he asks between laughs and breaths,
"What's wrong, Charlie Brown?"

Through sobs and half-chokes, salty tears that I don't remember tasting,
can't remember tasting –
I try to say –
maybe I don't say?
But in my head, I know –
"Grandpa, you can't be here.
Don't you know you're dead?"

My grandfather never owned a red baseball cap.

My cousins,
more brothers than cousins – constant and annoying and protective, like when they chased me into the woods, threatening handfuls of dock spiders, and then chased away the stray dog that barked and growled at me –

wore baseball caps, Toronto Blue Jays and Michigan State.
They used to throw me from the dock every summer,
to test for muskies.

There are no muskies in Stoney Lake.
They were story-creatures that man fought up North –
monsters my grandfather made up
to frighten small children from swimming alone.
Great fish with teeth!

But even northwards there were no muskies:
in Deer Lake, walleye and jackfish populate instead.

To filet them is to carve them:
to slice down the cheek and along the backbone,
to plunge past the ribs
and rip skin from tail to head.

After three hours of cutting fish,
the white of your nails is crammed with grey,
scales find every crease and crack – every fissure in your clothes and flesh.
They hide in the joints of your fingers
and fly into your hair.
They taste like cold lake sand.

"Water connects the people," Lani told me around the campfire one day,
my thumbs aching from holding tails and peeling fish.
"We don't remember it, when the world was water,
when there were only boats instead of roads
and how we'd paddle just to see our neighbour.
Our grandfathers do not remember –
but the turtle does, the birds, the fish,
even the crocodiles, I reckon."
Lani looked at the spot beside the rocks,
where I had spilled the cooking oil,

blue veins swirling against the dark green drop,
"Now, the lakes and rivers are drying up, you know?
Who will remember when all the fish and turtles are gone?"

65.1 % of the human body is water,
70.8% of the Earth.
A kwe can go 30 days without food, but only 3 without a drink.

The night I dreamt of my grandfather, I woke to find my gran
    sitting in the kitchen –
grandpa's service picture and a bottle on the white, doily tablecloth.
"Nostalgia is like wine," my grandmother said, sipping
from a glass of dark merlot.
"A little bit and it's nice and sweet and warms you up. Too much
    and you risk

Drowning is a fire in the throat,
hot talons scratching at the back of your nose,
its splashes of light and slowed, frantic limbs
a sultry voice in your ear
to cease
to sink back into suspended animation
and slip past the dark below your feet.

I don't remember the drowning
I remember the panic
Maggie laughing, lake spray against our faces,
We were riding broncos that stole our breath,
Black tube bucking against St. Clair –

We caught the wake from the freighter at full speed,
flew for an instant – a weightless second of inner tube and sky,
Maggie's arm touched mine,
and then we hit
– plunged bellies first

flailing – seaweed water filling lungs
Coughing, sputtering
I remember the way the back of my nose stung.

Maggie pulled me up,
arms around my neck,
I thought she was screaming, but she was giggling when she said:
"Just stand up."

I don't remember the standing up. The water was only waist high.

Memories never freeze the same way twice,
some cold and hard and jagged –
icicles that slice through the thickest skin,
others—

I walk down Stella's road:
her Christmas present tucked under my arm,
her house in the distance,
snow swallows my knees,
air scrapes through my lungs when I breathe –
this is the road we ran down in the rain, the road that took up
summers walking from one end to the other, discussing Matt Malloy
and math class and nothing. This is the road I used to walk twice a day.

We're in the cold,
Stella and I,
sharing stories about grandfathers and drowning,
the sidewalk abides us, snow covered
and we're chatting, gabbing, babbling –

My grandfather is wearing that red baseball cap.
Floating on the divide between green lake and blue sky,
my grandfather is forever

laughing, Stella tells me that we'll always be
just two fools burning away our time, but
the polar icecaps are melting at rate of 9% each decade.

"Who will remember?"

When the sky begins to fall in fluffs,
we let
the snowflakes melt on our tongues.

Time Travel

These earrings
Take me back
To laughter
Warm grass
Lake air
Skies blue enough to fall into

When the fringe dances in the breeze
I forget to remember you
I expect you
In the next room over
Drinking coffee
Eating saltines
With butter

For a breath
You are here again
Denim, pony bead fringe
Clacking
As you wrap
A dripping six-year-old
In the safety
Of your worn jean jacket

Field Poem 1

Dream with me

A field
Lined by trees
Grey skies and a howling wind
Dancing spikes of stubborn, brittle grass
Earth hard, packed
Compressed
But waiting to swell

There is a house
Inside, you put wood into the stove
While children run
Through cramped spaces
Children, coiled like springs for the thaw
Ready to burst

You hear the agents before you see them
Engines turning, gravel crunching
A war time bugle

Fear hits you
Like a fishing hook threaded through the gut
Line taut
Pulling you into panic

You speak in verbs
Go.
Run.
Hide.

Now you are the child
Grass bones crunching as car doors open behind
You, running for the trees
Praying for the trees
Praying to melt into the land
Like frost in the morning sun

The agents come
Raiding
Yanking children from homes
Like weeds
And salting the earth

They leave mothers on porches
Toques on hooks
Books half-read
Games half-played

And yet

And yet

The land pulls back her ribbon skirt

Saplings
Become children again

(Plane Crash)

Panic is acidic, stomach-eating.

Panic envelops. A corrosive fog that sours synapses – heightening reaction, delaying animation, preparation.

The freefall was transmogrifying, displacing internal organs, making me feel with my eyeballs – eyeballs that couldn't scream, only watch as gravity pulled us in.

I wake to the smell of chemical fire – acrid and stinging my lungs.

Hindbrain and medulla driving now, I drag myself away. *I just want to sleep*, fade away into the cold embrace of snow, become water – join circles. Vapour, condensation, and liquid. Become molecules that drift and disperse …

I flail away from the crash site, sputter toward vacant space – space unmolested by the nosedive. *Is there such a thing?* (There is.) An expanse of bracing clarity, a mingling of known and unknown where breath leaves the body in familiar obfuscation. I pack the wound with stories and semaa and sweetgrass.

I see tracks of others, erratic – belongings and memories, memories of belonging lay scattered in the white. Behind me burns the wreckage of a fiction we told ourselves about the world. *I should find them*, I think – the survivors, I mean, but I don't, won't even try. The melancholy of survival is self-indulgent, only briefly peeking through the cloak of private degradation.

I pocket a piece of shrapnel. Sharp and jagged, useful in its violence. A promise of severing or masochism or self-defense. What endures subsists on well-worn paths – neural, emotional. Chemical markers to light the way back...

No.

I choose the expanse.

I tread through the snow – snow crunching against the pristine silence of the night. I stop, a preservation of the sharp quiet – quiet, cutting and encompassing. Cutting through the noise of isolation. This is the inviting silence of a world turned towards reflection, sleeping – in dreams – possibilities that might become ... winter night, white blanket, black sky. Silver dots and the bone of the moon shining, making day out of dark. Moonlight smells like frosted cedar; air sits crisp against my throat.

I do not trudge, not anymore. I hop – no, lope. I hope – no, I pad through the snow, pressing infinities of suspended water onto dreaming grass. Breath hot, to remind me of the cold – temporary justice, like these tracks I set down. Below the layered meaning of crystal cold, the marrow of ancestors will hold my footfalls for the next generations to come.

I'm searching.

I find footprints of waabooz, lackadaisical. Contours of rabbit feet slipping through silence, into interstitial space where cedar trees greet the snow, where silver becomes shadow, where green defies white – green to remind me that nothing is absolute. We must always return.

I want to taste those bitter needles, but there is no tea for this... there is only medicine of an inviting silence. Stark and still, and yet I still feel us clamoring. Making noise to fill the void, a severance of a world connected tangentially.

I do not follow the waabooz (this time). I choose a sublimation of wandering – no, searching. I am not lost; I am searching.

PULL

Axiology: A Paper

In Ikea, I meander
through elbows and inattention,
slices of homes like cake
suspended
just
long
enough
to induce FOMO

Swedish nomenclature forgiven
in the name of a deal:
baubles, monkeys, people

I hold a measuring tape and a list of numbers
a treasure map for the underworld
These are coordinates to particle board splendour

I make the mistake
of leaning on a counter
shooed away by a woman ogling candles
or maybe, plates?

A new horde approaches and I scuttle
crab-like into a nook
smartly organized,
sustainable, it says

The overflow
of bodies washes into
this tiny living playhouse
and I make my escape for a purple *sophisticated*
den

Empty, luxury living out of trend
a couch as big as a nook –
I give in, stretch out, knock over a plant.

I apologize
(to the plant)
blatant in my gracelessness
bend over vegan leather to pick her up
maybe I'll take her home in recompense
where she can sun herself in
the kitchen windowsill
away from the cat

I grope for her tiny home
Sorry, sorry, sorry.
She does not answer.

The plant is plastic.

Advice from my mother on a dreamwalk

Be loud
So the monsters will hear you

Carry kindness as contraband
Stow it away in secret pockets
So you can never be robbed of it

Tread heavily
So the world feels your steps

Break bones with your wit
Flash sharp words instead of fists
So silence can never starve you

Follow butterflies
So you forget the road

Flex anger like currency
Plant shackles to grow memory
Make blankets out of body bags

And,
If ensnared,
Offer wrath

My Mother's Buffet

Golden pine
That gawdy pine
Of my childhood

Meant for finery
China dishes, silver teaspoons

Where we stuffed receipts
And little toys
We didn't want to put away.

My mother pulls open
A drawer
Pens and paper clips
A sigh
A weathered photograph
Cheeks full, smiling
Is that you, or me?

I hid
My favourite VHS tape inside
The cabinet, once
So my brother
Couldn't
Wring the film out and offer it to the sun

Brass knobs, glass doors
Big drawer
At the bottom
That inevitably
Became
A sea of cords and Pokemon cards

We sat the tv on it
Made an altar out of gawdy pine
My mother would say
Kitsch will be in again
As if
The buffet
Had a chance at Rocky Horror glory

After her stroke
Her entropy
Filled
The vacant spaces of our house

My mother hated that buffet
Its kaleidoscope contents
Balking presence
She would decry
The cheap particle board
Its ugliness and disuse

I never learned
The origin story
Of my mother's nemesis

We renovated the house
Twice

Each time,
The buffet remained

Choke in the Throat

Rita Joe
You know
That talk
You lost

Was taken

Shingwauk
Mohawk
St. Joseph's Hospital
(Gitchimookman
Yellowhead Policy)

Took

Nokomisag
Mishomisag
That won't
Ever be

We grieve
Elders lost
That never
Got to breathe

I hate
The way
I choke
On words

Sorry
Is not
My family's
Story

Rita Joe
We know
We are not
"Trauma"

These nouns
(Shaagnaash sounds)
Make static
Songs
I want to – no,
Will (one day)
Sing

Gambian Peanut Soup

You tell me the soup is too hot
For Canadian tastebuds

I remind you
Canada
Has little sway over my palate

My tastebuds are Anishinaabe, Kanien'keha'ka
Generations of fireweed and sumac
Hardened

Ok, you say
Stirring ground nuts and chilis
"I'll make this Gambian then"

Good,
Because Canada is not ethnicity
But citizenship
Canada is border
Drawn by rich white men

And you laugh,
Because the Gambia knows all too well
About white men's borders
Their need, their trade carving lines into maps
Turning English into currency

You speak five languages.
Wow, you say.
Ha.
Oui.

But you came to these borders
Just as I was born in them
Less than

Soup is made for stories, you tell me
So I share mine
And when I'm done, you'll smile

"We'll honour your ancestors then"
Choosing squash
Instead of sweet potato

And I choose to tell you
How sweet potato
Was carried across the Atlantic
By those same white men

"Turtle Island claims my soup," you say
"She can share it with Africa"

But this *is* Gambian.
Vibrant, immemorial, unrelenting

And when we eat
The soup is hot as the Gambian sun

Hollowpoint Indifference

I am not untouched, unscathed. I am not lucky.

True, the bullet didn't rip through me, but I was in the room.

We are all in the same room. Glass shatters. Blood sprays.
We are all in the same room.

It will be okay. Everything will be okay.

Okay is a state that only exists in the future.

Okay is the horizon our fingers grope for each morning as the sun breaks open the sky and we see just how far away we are from okay.

Okay left my friend to be found by his landlady, lying on the carpet of his apartment.

Okay assumes patchwork where gaping holes rest instead. Gaping like it was some surprise—

Okay pulls the trigger, pops the pills, fills a glass.

We are scathed. We are all scathed. (We are all in the same room.)

I/we sat in the hospital, scathing. I/we waited for the phone call, scathing. I/we slept the day away scathing.

I/we reside in the furthest state from unmolested the English language will allow. This is not okay.

We are all in the same room, diving for cover and covering each other.

We are hugging each other to survive, holding each other's existence against the velocities of hollow point indifference, eardrums exploding at each cacophony of silence as yet another body hits the floor.

We are not lucky to avoid the violence, not lucky in ~~wearing~~ carrying others' blood.

We are not occupiers of okay, nor pilgrims of okay.

Okay, I/we realize, is white. Okay is capitalism. Okay is maintenance. Perpetuity. Homeostasis.

Okay sets us up for failure the moment the incantation is voiced. It will never be okay, because the criteria for okay lies in a morgue, in a ditch, in a river *as we speak*.

We are all in that morgue, ditch, river …

We are all holding each other in that morgue, ditch, river – washing clothes and bodies, picking bullet fragments out of our hair.

We will not be okay.

We refuse.

I wake

Is this sleeping?
We ask to breathe
With knees on our necks
Yearn for futures
Where our children
Do not lay hidden in the ground
This is a world where logic rolls in on itself
A mobius strip of reason
We tread water in the wake of freighters
Cargo ships carrying truth & justice for someone else

I know there have been dreams
But, we must dream with our eyes open
Visionary, but vigilant
Pupils dilated
Hands becoming fists
So that our defiance becomes a forest
Immutable, stalwart

Let me be clear
We choose the waking
The walking, the marching
Footsteps punctuating survival
Footsteps loud, to wake others

I wake
I am waking buds
Becoming shoots, becoming trees
Crumbling sidewalk
Shattering concrete with my reach

Wait. No, I wade
Through
Manufactured confusion
Demeaning origins: Lead Belly, Erykah Badu
Reforging morals: waking is not politics
Waking is a state of being
Waking is

But this,
This is a wake of reason
Collecting grief and names in a book
Look upon this spackled corpse
Do you feel included yet?
Cheeks painted with beautiful words
Adorned in Walmart slogans
This isn't death, the sign says
This is transformation.

Forget the soundbites.
The white noise
Static like a blanket
Muffling our voices

We tear through
Turning static into music
Blankets into beats
Footsteps
Do you hear them?
Do you see
The water, trembling in the glass?
We are waking

To wake is to see
Gain sight of the unsightly
See the sharks
Before they attack
Because there is blood in the water
(There is always blood in the water)

I wake with you
We wake
We shake the sleep from your eyes
Show you the fins among the waves
Grow wildwood with our fingers clenched

And those who choose to sleep?

Those who fear the waking
Do so
Because the nightmare serves them

Plough Depth

I hear them stutter
Anish-nishin-naabek
O-nay-da
Lu-nop-pe-wak?
Obligatory
Like a wave from the queen

We sit and listen
Polite
Crowd forgiving
Waiting for the box to check

An auntie whispers,
We've only been here for 10 000 years, and they can't say our names yet?

Speech acts flagrant
We acknowledge
The violence of stakes and claims
One reconciling pat on the back

So, how deep do these acknowledgements go?
Maybe six feet?

The institution workshops
Sterilized words
Bronzed garden nameplates
To tread upon

Reconciliation churns the topsoil
But keeps the mineral rights of our oppression

What are they afraid of?
The grenades they left in the ground, at Ipperwash?

They tried to erase us so deep

They tried to erase us so deep
It took ground penetrating radar to illuminate the shadow of
Canada the Destroyer
215 tiny bodies
Unearthed
A truth that had been buried alive

Thrashing, those memories
Clawing the insides of spirit and mind, heart and body
We hear you; we never stopped listening.
We did not forget you.

Trauma is not defined by a lack of documentation
"Hearsay," whispers
The degradation of physical evidence
Omission …
Or records kept guarded beyond white walls

When truth goes missing by the thousands …
Becoming a presence of absence
Looking away becomes national policy
Comforting, cleanly etched into the conscience of the pristine
True North, Strong and Free

They were children.

They expunged (our) lives from the record
Rubbed them out so enthusiastically
That the documents hold holes
Deep as graves

State of Being

A landfill
A river
A ditch

We are searched for (not searched for)
Found (not found)
Photographs
Like tombstones

Neither alive
Nor dead

Missing is an after-image
Burned onto retinas
Blink
We persist
There (not there)
Evidence
Like moonlight

Missing is an abyss
No body, no crime
A statehood of gnawing
Constant shadow in the corner of the eye

I walk the park
Red dresses hung in trees
To the present
Who know only *alive* or *dead*
Their eyes
View ornaments

They cannot see
The space
Between
Smile and memory

Tree Museum

There is no grieving process
For the tall ones lost
To the imposition of strangers
Remaking their strange lands
Silent invasions, planted
Seeds from across the sea

A cookie cut-out displayed,
Four feet wide
My friend puts his hand upon smoothed rings
I knew this tree

Ornamentation stifling first beings
While cities raze whole communities
(Scot's Pine was not the remedy
Wild parsnip, a poison)

We need good guests, my Uncle reminds me
Lilacs, an allegory for
Coexisting

We need kitigan
Not subdivisions
Seed nurseries
To reconcile
Artifacts of giants
We put on walls

Field Poem 2

Field muck,
A memory I never lived
Land, my feet never touched
Stirs
Sweet, wild grass, pink clover, cedar and pine
A swath of ancestry
A homestead

I sleep as the frogs do
In mud
I smell cedar and pine through my skin
Carried on cold snaps
Scent, sitting in my cells
A seed
To bring me home

I sing as the crows do
Raw, irregular
An arrythmia
Of roots
Tangling wings
Confused

Yet I drifted away
Caught on cottonwood fluffs
Or

Unplanted,
I forgot the field
Forgot dreaming frogs and stalks of citizen grass
The calls of crows ricocheting against sentinel trees
Could not recall the spectacle
Of Riverlands
I grew
Under different clouds
Thinking
I was the bark and needles of cedar alone

The squish returns me
Re-members me

The trees wake
Cedar and pine
I stir
Dreaming of feet
Sinking into the sop
My feet
Finding homestead soil
Re-seeding
As plants do

LOOSE

Deshkan Ziibing Wiingashk

This city, Deshkan Ziibi:
The French and English delighted in
The confluence, the people (Chonnonton, Nishnaabeg)
Muddy waters breaking trade
Simcoe wanted capital, pursuing rivers for circulation
Watershed – arteries and veins

Turtles sun themselves on
Rocks pushed by glaciers along a waterway erased as
"Thames", skirting shadows of
Overpasses, carapace a calendar, scales warming, warming blood
Horns blare up above, inconsequential
Traffic misery unknown
To mishiikenh

I sit in an Uber, late by a measure not found on turtle shells.
Roads congested, we smother the asphalt
I am stuck, a passenger, Wharncliffe glacial
Turtles sunning, geese irreverent on the Forks
Stuck on antler tines, this city
Is velvet, not bone

The banks of Deshkan Ziibi buttress urban bulge, I
Wonder about mnoomin, if shores sang in the imprecise
Wind, grains threshed for humans, rivers
Knock me from this bridge
A gentle tap, falling, gathered in canoes
Sweet with maple syrup, venison

Stewing, my driver smacks the steering wheel
Angry for the sitting, idle in a construct in a construct.
These roads were made; these traffic lights were made;
London the city, Deshkan Ziibi the place
Artifice begets hubris, these roads were paved
To rewrite the Land

I crack the window enticing ziigwan air, rush
Of Gold and pollen, I used to fear the sacrament of sneezing,
Grass-allergen-Indian-litmus-test
Antihistamines imbue foreigner status, a pill
To play act belonging, convoluting an incongruent
Self, snipping rootedness like weeds

I used to sink into myself, sink into the
Safety of self, confinement and definition drawn by
City limits, ever one degree removed, displaced:
Territory, language, Indigeneity –
Put "urban" in front to separate
Foremost, you are the city

You don't find out without looking
Extrinsically the city grass
Imported, lawns irk immune systems, not
Belonging, never found in Anishinaabemowin
Or on greening Deshkan Ziibi shores, our bodies
Remain catalogues of Antler River ecology

In a car, on a road the city wants you to forget
Coyote and Raccoon, Waabooz and Waawaashkesh
How Falcons redefine skyscrapers, building
Aerie, fuzzy babies urban, wild
Indigenous nations of sinew of natural
(metropolitan) Watershed,

Nature is the constant, city superimposed
Deshkan Ziibi adamantine, London limits do not stop
River flows, through the window (in the traffic)
Through a crack of freedom,
Me escaping (construct within a construct)
Sweetgrass finds me

Water trails unrelenting, turtles articulating
Our relationship with the sun, the wiingashk stirs, sweet
Like nationhood, medicine breeze
Impervious to concrete or definitions.
Breath of sovereignty, it reminds me
There are no City Indians, only Indian cities.

Coyotesong

I hear them
from within the dark
calling, haunting

Coyote singers
reclaiming urban earth

They rally
voices chasing voices
night laughter
braiding into
one
long
howl
preparing for the hunt

Limbic notes that
touch hairs on the back
of your neck

Like the chill of dew on bare feet
slick & cold & sharp
against skin

Like the heat of adrenaline
fight & flight & epinephrine
through veins

Where grass and tarmac collide
the wild music
makes
its
way
in

One song at a time

Wiingashk Sunlight

I am stuck in my body
Mapping territories, rupture and renewal
Tracing topographies
Relating echoes of raindrops, seismic upheaval
Tectonic histories interlaced with waking buds
Knee-deep in three rivers – what has, what will, what is
I am cosmology, you say
I am universe, scattered as loose defiance
Down the side of a mountain that
The wolves climb to converse with the moon
Sweet as wiingashk sunlight
These scars mark a highway of stories
Holding me
I *am* a cosmology of wounds
Complexities sutured with semaa
Picking at scabs
Tearing open holes in the sky that
Arrows of geese escape from

Where we converge

I begin
where we all begin
as water

Molecules
finding one another through the chaos of the universe
condensing
becoming clouds –
gravity's gentle hands
pulling us back to Earth

We do not sublimate
(even the hardest of us melts)

When I join the lake,
I become the lake
and
the lake becomes me
We converge and divulge

In this cycle of becoming, joining and returning, the questions
gain scales and fins
and slip –
away

Words become vapour

I end as we all end
as water,

What the land asks of us

The seed does not ask
The earth
To embrace it
Does not ask
The rains
To shower it
Does not beseech
The sun to warm the ground

I put ideas
Into a bank account
So that we can eat
Property plus productivity
A calculation
For determining worth
I pay deductions
For skin color, upbringing, postal code

Outside
The math is simple

Vultures circle
A macabre round dance
Cleaning bones
So that roadkill
Takes on meaning

Without
The cement and picket fences
Our deaths
Become something else

Sun dried bones
Feed soil
So that heart berries
Might poke red
Amidst the bramble and foreigner grass
Of discarded land

Field jewels
Whose worth
Is a calculation
Of sweetness and sustenance

Strawberries do not ask
To propagate
Birds, beaks red with juice
Spread seeds
Bees carry their gold
Mixing pistils and stamens
The sun warms the green
Of the sprout
So that light becomes fruit

Land
Is treaty
Continuance
Responsibility

When we find
The field berries
Our fingers red with summer nectar
They do not ask
If we are worthy
They ask to be eaten.

Muskrat Teachings

These Bkejwanong shores
Do not concede

Sand becomes silt becomes water
Slopping, lapping, crashing
Against freighters in the Great Lakes' sun

In the twilight
St. Clair gleams
Stars set in headlights and porch lanterns

Across the water
Algonac beckons
Close-far, relative-stranger, international

In the dark
The muskrats show us
The foolishness
Of marking waterways as borders

They glide across the silver
Shore to shore
laughing

The Castle

We know the promise
Institution as beacon
This tower, a lighthouse
Where bright minds shine

We know the dream
Painting futures in three dimensions
The vibrancy of our murals
Undiluted

I walk the halls
Incognito in plain sight
Enrollment, an insurgency
Leaving brushmarks in my wake

We follow the dream, not the promise
Treading schools built like castles

Institution as bastion
Hulking gates and hewn stone parapets
To remind
This is not for everyone

We remember
When schooling was a knife
Dissecting families
Carving people into slivers

Making good citizens out of bad Indians

We sit in classrooms
With our ancestors
Drawing spirit lines
Connecting forward and back

Education like graffiti
Scrawling blueprints
Across ivory walls

For siege towers

To the wolf spider in my garden

You are the monarch I failed to attract
Planting milkweed
Growing bush clover
I put down cedar chips
To cover clay that barely holds grass
Found endemic seeds on Etsy
Envisioning
Stained glass wings
Orange and black

Dear spider,
Maybe you'll laugh
At the futility
Of growing wildflowers in planters
Alienating natives
With dirt from a bag

We build butterfly causeways
Hoping to bridge
Our excuses
A strip of untamed greenery
Offered
Patting ourselves on the back,
We bravely rewrite bylaw
Replacing Kentucky blue
With Indiangrass

Dear predator,
I did not dream of hairy legs
Skittering in the creeping vines
My app cannot identify
You didn't dream of homelessness
Exodus from the trees and brush

What design
Compelled spiders to diaspora?
Was it the calamity of EV factories, or
Detached residential sprawl?
Single families need development
Stores to buy soil from

Meanwhile
ER rooms decry
Wolf bites, lacking anti-venom

We Rescue Dogs

We rescue dogs –
Posting pictures on Instagram
Wearing t-shirts adorned with slogans and paw prints
Making jobs out of cruelty

We rescue dogs –
From cities overrun by humanity
Dusty streets as seen on Facebook
Far far away

We bring dogs home –
Into houses we can't afford
Onto streets where we build speed bumps
So that our cars don't kill children

I brought a dog home –
All 5.6 pounds
Ribs poking out
Abandoned, or escaped from a puppy mill

She is larger than the world will allow
Forgives without stipulation
Waits for me to eat
Will charge mastiffs to protect the ones she loves

Each summer
We lose lives
To an ignorance of rivers and lakes
She remembers how to swim before toes ever touch water

We rescue dogs,
Affecting noblesse oblige
But what we think makes us more
Makes us lesser instead

Coming back to the round dance

Spring rain
Sweet smell of waning winter
Cold mist and warm cheeks
A circle of feet and ribbon skirts

Shoulders close
Close enough to feel each other's laughter
Closeness when we've been so far apart
Flush with distance

Masks off
Seeing faces for their smiles
This orbit
Familiar and brand new

We start untethered, disjointed
Unsure
Dancing ellipses
Me, stumbling

I can't find the rhythm when we don't hold hands

So, in the mist
We become the circle
A conjunction of hearts
Courting Equinox

Breath hot
Drum beats like the sun
Pulling us close
In step
Scatter us, we return
To the circle
To the drum
To each other

Starlight Tour

I wish I could have walked with you
Spilled open the night
Like a fish
Fed you with stories
As gravel crunched

I know you walk
With hands in pockets
Hands clenched
Holding on
Holding in

I would
Stir the asters in the indigo fields
Knit you a blanket with their petals
Weave songs into the wind

This solitude
Cold and brittle
Imposed
Designed
So that you fade into the night

I wish I could have walked with you
Cobbled boots
Out of strips of laughter
Raced you home
As snow fell

That one about coyote-wolf and the spring flowers

I lope through cold mud, coaxing
Seeds to grow, breaking trail with
Hardened feet, claws like moonstone
That pull tides of clouds across
Crescent nightscapes to bathe
In rays of burrowed sun. Untethered
I am not the city, not the wild
But the truth between the two, the hyphen
Holding worlds together, my body
A bridge the squirrels use to replant
Forests, my voice a coruscation
Of fireflies waiting for the summer
Heat, my nose moist in the frost-
Turned dew, imbibing hints of dinosaurs
Unfound and future histories
Unwritten. I chase the ancestors
In the sky, moving stars with a howl, dart
After seasons within a cadence that
Tracks raindrops onto melting lakes,
Correlates circles that extend
Like helixes escaping the sun, painting
Auroras in the blossoms my tracks stir
To bloom

Primitive Language

We say "primitive", place time
And distance between words,
Separation softens mountains, we lose (the point)
Forgetting etymology, we say primitive hear *quaint*
Primitive people, incomplex, we
Instantiate simple, not First People, we
Invalidate the sophistication of primitive bows
If you're going to bring a bow to the hunt, bring
The one that started it all;

I struggle, scrawling amidst nations
Loud with storytellers, orators
Our knowledge
Lives in syllables, enunciated
Syllables gathered in community, sharing whole
Cosmologies
One verb
At a time, our knowledge is
Memengwaa, the Land, our chrysalis

But I pin down words
Performing lepidoptery
These sentences
Shadow boxes
Fingertips meticulous, trying not to
Tear wings in the process

Translucent, light behaves as a particle
And a wave, metaphysical or metamorphic, or maybe self-aware
These words attempting metabolism, poly-
Synthetic storying too intricate for the
Incomplexity of nouns

I need primitive language
Minwaajim (*to tell good stories*)
Niin gikendam debwewin ayaa (*I know the truth is*)
Zhaaganaashiimowin bwaa-gashkinaan (*English cannot hold*)
Anishinaabemowin ezhi-izhijiwan *(the way the Anishinaabe language flows)*

In my mother's, grandmother's tongue
Cadence is circadian
Wings oscillate waveform, the scintillation of sunshine,
The way the ferns flicker on bright days

I am unpinning butterflies (metaphorically)
Minwaajim
Berry-picking, miinan nestled
Among stones and juniper, coaxing waaboozoog
To tell me how to make
Miini-baashkiminasigani-biitoosijigani-bakwezhigan
Not "blueberry pie"

Letter to a father I never got to know

I remember you in flashes
You are lightning
Filling rooms of my childhood
Brilliant, brief

A sandbox
A phone call
An armful of presents left on the porch
Your voice

You called me warrior
Before I knew I had to fight
Two fingers for victory
Because peace comes at a price

I look for you
In my smile
(One dimple)
Feel your anger in mine
Dark, Hollywood Indian hair
Coarse and wild

I sit with your absence
Listening
For words across space and time

Did my absence feel
Like the negative of a photograph?

I inherited
Sarcasm
Obstinance
The hackles of a wolf

Field Poem 3

Sunlight
In the homestead field
Finds you
Unfaltering
Bright fingers – warm like hard work
Beading sweat across brows

Wild grasses and clover converse
On this ancestral ground, I feel tangential
Like fiddleheads,
Questions curling
Inwards

My cousin makes bows
Shows me how two fingers draw velocities with a snap
Warns me of the learning curve
The flesh sacrifice
To fly an arrow shaft
Hands me a bow, hand-forged from ash

I teach all the cousins, and they pick it up quick.

Fumbling,
I doubt my lineage
Athleticism articulated by a limp arrow on the grass

How do we return?
I feel tangential
Touching bows
Two points – the making of the bow, the loosing of the arrow
Then, diverging

Arrows wobble in the air
Too fast to see
Nanda-gikendam
Seeking—

I am looking for the person that comes after
The skin behind the scab

Sunlight, an interrogation
No dark spaces to shrink into

Auntie nudges bravery out of me
My cousin doesn't laugh
Persistence a callus

I do not intersect (just yet)
I am a line, a ray aiming for the
Curvature of the bow, shallow parabola of the arrow
As though the formula of the tangent
Might mark coordinates for
Return

In homestead sun
We draw stances
Immemorial

A bowstring
Pulled back
Dilates time

Shadows might be ancestors
Silhouettes the land knows
Of hunts—

Bodily
I am in the sun
On the field
Standing with
My cousin
Auntie and Uncle near
Drawing sinew back

Muscles forget/remember
Tension of anticipation, breath, shoulders taut—

How do we return?
Is it in the bow, or the arrow?

Rejoining trajectories, a practice of geometry
Solvable, yet
In the sun
On the field
Our blood recalls
Not formula, but
Relationship, between
Fingers and fletching
Breath and arrow
Body and bow
Cousins, aunties, uncles

I let go

The arrow flies
Tearing flesh
From my finger

Fiddleheads unfurl
In the sun

Indian Acts

A play of forbidden acts

ACT I

Tonight we're going to potlatch like it's 1875
Wear regalia to the club
Dance intertribal
Play bingo in Nish

Tonight we're going off the reservation
Without a pass
We'll keep our children and our names
Use farm equipment
Enter pool halls
(Just to leave again)

Tonight we're going to live
Even though
"Indians" weren't meant to last

ACT II

You hear the one about enfranchisement?
A doctor, a lawyer and a teacher walk into a bar,
No longer Indians.

ACT III

Let's have a pow wow while we hold the fort
Call all the chiefs in
Circle the wagons
To protect our dances
From the prying eyes of the ignoble and tame

We'll charge admission
Demand one quarter proof of
Settler blood

We'll steal the prime minister
Or maybe,
Make for Ottawa
But land in William's Lake

ACT IV

I have reservations
Thoughts restless
Corralled, like
Wild horses gathered for slaughter

Reconciliation
As a question
Provokes knee jerk reactions
Driving spurs into sides
To canter past interrogation

Show jumps like buffalo jumps
Earn accolades
While real reckoning
Rots in the sun

Teepees on campuses—
When we lived in wiigwam
A federal holiday like asphalt
Over grassroots events
A sea of orange shirts that
Drowns us out

Where are our children?

But we hired more natives
Added D to the end of EDI
Said our land acknowledgements
At every meeting

Still, I remember the
Horses slain
So Indians could not ride them

ACT V

The truth about status is
It's all made up
What registers as Indian
Expedites elimination

Follow the father
Remove the mother
Create conditionals
Stringent and straining

Birth year a variable
Laid out across
A careful spreadsheet of
Quantum thresholds, and

Diminishing returns—
Fulfilling Scott's
Dream
Of a vanishing race

Indian status is a numbers game

ACT VI

These seats are taken
War party of three

We had the audacity
To save up for a legal fund
Hold peaceful protest
On our land
Thinking (radically)
That human rights applied to Indians

A doctor, a lawyer, a teacher
(Still Lunaapeew, Onkwehon:we, Anishinaabe)
Ready their red hands
To plant Monsanto-free corn, write pre-emptive
Litigation, Yellowhead papers
Apply injunctions
Against the Government of Canada

So, tonight we're tearing up the treaties
(Tomorrow, you can leave)
Reaffirming
Miikinaak Minising ezhi-wiinde ow aki
Giidinawendimin, miinwaa
Debenjiged giimiingona dedbinwe wi naagdowendiwin.

Nanda-Gikendawin (*The Seeking*)

To me, all poetry is a search – we look within our Selves and without to find those truths the world needs to hear. One of my truths is that I was born Melissa Schnarr, not Melissa Powless or Melissa Day because my mother was stolen in the Sixties Scoop. My first chapbook, *Secondhand Moccasins*, was published under the name I was given within this legacy of stealing and transplanting children. This name still has value and meaning to me, but in offering my seeking and my truths in this collection, and onwards, I am rewriting my Self too, reclaiming who I was always meant to be.

Many Indigenous people across Turtle Island, and beyond, are in this place of seeking and reclaiming. Settler colonialism has worked for generations to sever us from the places, people and nations to which we belong. I am not alone. You are not alone. We are all coming home.

During the development of *A Bow Forged from Ash*, I began to (re)learn one of my languages, Anishinaabemowin, which lives in me through my mother's side of my family. My great-grandmother, Wanaasin-ba (*Lavina-ba Day*), was a fluent speaker of

Anishinaabemowin, but our beautiful and vibrant language was stripped from my family through the Residential School system. I am reclaiming it for myself and everyone behind me, syllable by syllable. This is another truth of mine: Anishinaabemowin nda kinomaagwos. (*I am learning Anishinaabemowin*). My community's dialect, Bkejwanonging Anishinaabemowin, mixes Ojibwe and Pottawatomi forms, showing us our history – how the Pottawatomi joined the Ojibwe people who lived in Chigamiin Aki (*Great Lakes area*), travelling north into what is understood as Canada, rather than be pushed West by the US Indian policies of the time. My Anishinaabemowin is not perfect or fluent but my use of it in this collection is truthful. It is a textual and linguistic marker of where I am in my reclamation journey and I will not be ashamed of that!

Miigwetch to you for reading and sitting with my truths. If you are also on a path of reclamation, know that we are walking beside each other. There are no maps for this journey and it can be as hard as sharp gravel on soft, winter feet, but we will walk at our own pace and we will learn to see so many things that have been left for us by those who came before us. As my language teacher has told me, "Pick it all up."

In zaagidiwn and solidarity,

Melissa Powless Day

Notes

"Moccasin Poem":

This is a 're-tread' of "Stone Hammer Poem" by Robert Kroetsch, originally published 1975.

"Field Poem 1":

Some children managed to escape and hide from the Indian Agents, but many did not.

"Starlight Tour":

Starlight Tours are a Canadian police practice wherein Indigenous people (often men) are taken into custody for public intoxication or public disturbance, then driven out of the city limits in sub-zero temperatures and left to find their way back. This practice dates back as early as 1976 and as recently as 2023. To date, not one police officer has ever been convicted for their role in the freezing deaths of these Indigenous people.

Acknowledgements

"Bezhgoozhi" was previously published in *The New Quarterly.*

"Rough Cut" was previously published in the *Yellow Medicine Review.*

"They tried to erase us so deep" and "Where we converge" were previously published in *The Temz Review.*

"Northern Lights," "Moccasin Poem," "Displace," "Refraction," "This is not a discovery," "Blood Memory," and "(Plane Crash)" were previously published in *Secondhand Moccasins* (Anstruther Press, 2023).

Miigwetch and Nia:wen

Chi-miigwetch, nia:wen to everyone who helped me develop this collection. I say *develop* because, really, the writing of these poems was one of the last steps in a particularly arduous learning trek, oftentimes thick with the clarity of mud or solemn like a winter moon or exhausting like a swim for your life.

Thank you to everyone who taught me, listened to me, read drafts or asked questions or who just sat in silence with me.

I didn't know it at the time, but the first step of creating this collection was always going to be about getting to know the Land, re-introducing myself to Deshkan Ziibi, Bkejwanong and the Grand River, among so many other powerful places within the basin of the Great Lakes.

Miigwetch to the Indigenous Writers' Circle at Western, to Rachelle Coleman, David Monture and Tom Cull for your ever-ready support and open hearts. Miigwetch to Brent Debassige; in guiding me on how to be a good scholar, you've also helped me become a better poet. Nia:wen to Auntie Jackie and Uncle Ron for your thoughts, wisdom, stories. Nia:wen to

Malcolm for teaching a cousin how to shoot a bow. Nia:wen to January Rogers for the big aunty energy you exude and for what you see in me, even when I don't. Miigwetch to Eshkiniigijik Ni'aankenimaagedaa Anishinaabemnaa. Miigwetch to Jaach, Paige and Giizhgaandak and to my fellow language learners for teaching me how to 'pick it all up'. Miigwetch to HayLee for getting a cousin to class.

Miigwetch, nia:wen to Jim Johnstone, my patient editor, and Aimee Parent Dunn, at Palimpsest Press for your support and belief in this collection.

Miigwetch, nia:wen to all those who came before me. Miigwetch nimaamaa, *Meggan Schnarr-Rice* (Margaret Sword) for starting this journey for both of us. Miigwetch, nia:wen, anushiik Deshkan Ziibi miinwaa Chigamiin Aki for your beauty, strength and knowledge and for sustaining us. Miigwetch Pixie waabandam niin. Gda chiminobizidamed.

Melissa Powless Day is Anishinaabe and Kanien'kehá:ka from Bkejwanong Territory (Walpole Island First Nation), with family ties in Six Nations of the Grand River Territory. She is a writer, scholar and educator who is currently pursuing a PhD in Indigenous Education at Western University. She also serves as the chair for Western's Indigenous Writers' Circle and as a Visiting Cultural Teacher for the London District Catholic School Board. Her work has appeared in the *Temz Review, The New Quarterly, The Windsor Review, Luna Station Quarterly* and *Yellow Medicine Review*. Her first poetry chapbook, *Secondhand Moccasins*, was published in 2023 by Anstruther Press and short-listed for the bpNichol Chapbook Award. She lives in Deshkan Ziibi (London, Ontario) with her research assistants, Pixie the chihuahua and Shiloh, the orange tabby.